The
Value Guide
To
ANTIQUE OAK FURNITURE

by

Conover Hill

Price Update
1978-1979

COLLECTOR BOOKS
Box 3009
PADUCAH, KENTUCKY 42001

INTRODUCTION

In the past several years, oak furniture has become a very collectible item throughout the United States. The good solid oak pieces that were so popular from 1850-1930 have won the hearts of thousands of avid collectors and have become useful in today's home furnishings. Several factors are responsible for the resurrection of oak; first, the wood itself is very durable, lending itself admirably to refinishing and restoring. Second, today's collector can associate himself and his childhood with the many pieces of oak furniture that he grew up with. Third, oak furniture is still available in the antique shops, flea markets, auctions and sales at a reasonable cost.

Oak, at the turn of the century, was the furniture manufacturers' dream. It could be produced and transported in mass, with the huge oak forests of the South and Midwest producing millions of board feet of lumber each year. The lumber could be kiln dried and used almost immediately from the saw log. With direct steam, the wood could be formed, curved, pressed and designed. Because of these advantages, oak furniture became the favorite of middle-class America.

The manufacturers used many phrases to describe the attributes of oak furniture in their ads: "Oak, as you know, is the finest of all cabinet hardwoods"...."Oak has a tough grain, is strong and lasting and lends itself to more permanent and rigid construction"...."You never have to be afraid of marring or scratching the finish as it will stand-up under the hardest of use"...."Made of the most durable wood known, Indiana quarter-sawn golden oak".

The quarter-sawn log, a method to expose the grain rays running from the heart to the bark, was a more expensive process because it necessitated more handling, entailed more loss than conventional cutting and required larger saw logs. The illustration here demonstrates both the quarter-sawn and the conventional methods. Note the medullary rays on the quarter sawn log as opposed to the straight grain of the conventional-sawn logs.

Plain and Quarter Sawn Oak

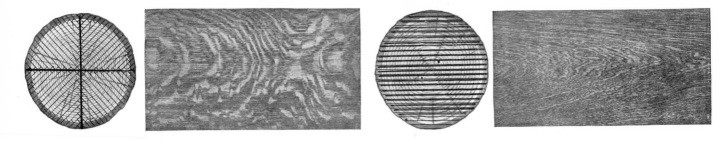

White oak was touted to be the very finest of all the different oaks used; however, very little was used since it was already bringing a premium in the barrel industry. White oak staves are the very finest and as far as I know, are still the only staves used in the manufacture of whiskey barrels.

PRICING

The most difficult task in publishing a book on furniture is arriving at a representative figure that will be accepted in all sections of the country. We took a sample of prices from many sources in several different locations in order to average an acceptable price. Factors considered in the pricing of this book include: condition, quality, solid wood vs. veneer, ornamentation, cost of restoration and the results of actual sales of oak pieces. THE PRICES IN THIS BOOK REPRESENT THE RETAIL PRICE RANGE THAT A DEALER MIGHT ASK FOR A FULLY RESTORED AND REFINISHED PIECE OF OAK FURNITURE IN HIS SHOP. We must take into consideration the different costs such as caning, upholstering, repairing, rebuilding, refinishing, and other costs that add up when bringing a piece of furniture to a perfect state. Take into consideration also that a dealer must make a reasonable profit after he has put his time and money in it.

Generally speaking, solid woods command a higher price than the veneers; however, oak veneers can be bought and applied with a little time and experience.

The Victorian pieces with their ornate carvings of lions heads, claw feet, oak leaves and other fancy decorations are much in demand and command a very high price. Most of these pieces were not mass produced and were quite costly during the era in which they were manufactured.

We hope that you will use this book as a price guide and a reference and not as a set price system. Prices will vary in different sections of the country and will fluctuate with each passing month. Enjoy the book, take it with you to shows, auctions and shops. I'm sure you will find it to be an invaluable aid in your search for collectible oak furnishings.

BEDS

The prices in this book represent the retail price range that a dealer might ask for a fully restored and refinished piece of oak furniture.

200.00-225.00

190.00-210.00

200.00-225.00

375.00-400.00

175.00-195.00

BEDS

The prices in this book represent the retail price range that a dealer might ask for a fully restored and refinished piece of oak furniture.

275.00-295.00

325.00-350.00

150.00-175.00

250.00-275.00
Pressed Cane
headboard &
footboard.

375.00-400.00

BEDS

275.00-295.00

475.00-525.00

250.00-275.00

250.00-275.00
Mahogany Wood
Sometimes Oak Wood

FOLDING BEDS

Folding beds, or Murphy beds, are large, heavy pieces. They are relatively scarce, and in years to come could become collectors items.

450.00-495.00

500.00-550.00

500.00-550.00

400.00-450.00

525.00-575.00

450.00-495.00

6

FOLDING BEDS

The prices in this book represent the retail price range that a dealer might ask for a fully restored and refinished piece of oak furniture.

525.00-575.00

525.00-575.00

500.00-550.00

525.00-575.00

475.00-525.00

500.00-550.00

550.00-594.00

425.00-475.00

525.00-575.00

500.00-550.00

BOOK CASES

The prices in this book represent the retail price range that a dealer might
ask for a fully restored and refinished piece of oak furniture.

425.00-450.00
Sectional Bookcase

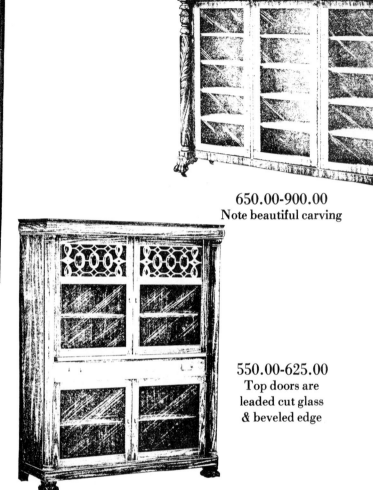

650.00-900.00
Note beautiful carving

550.00-625.00
Top doors are
leaded cut glass
& beveled edge

1400.00-1700.00
Carved Northwind
drawer pulls
(Museum Quality)

475.00-525.00

BOOK CASES

The prices in this book represent the retail price range that a dealer might
ask for a fully restored and refinished piece of oak furniture.

175.00-195.00

200.00-225.00

225.00-275.00

225.00-250.00

225.00-275.00

275.00-325.00

450.00-500.00

225.00-250.00

300.00-350.00
Desk/Bookcase
Sectional

BOOK CASES

400.00-450.00

325.00-375.00
Sectional Bookcase

300.00-375.00
5 Sections

Detail of Assembly
for sectional
bookcase

BUFFETS (sideboards)

250.00-275.00

250.00-275.00

225.00-250.00

250.00-275.00

225.00-250.00

225.00-250.00

BUFFETS (sideboards)

425.00-475.00

425.00-475.00

525.00-575.00

425.00-450.00

250.00-295.00

250.00-275.00

225.00-250.00

200.00-225.00

275.00-325.00

BUFFETS (sideboards)

The prices in this book represent the retail price range that a dealer might ask for a fully restored and refinished piece of oak furniture.

500.00-550.00
Leaded glass doors

500.00-550.00
Leaded glass doors

450.00-495.00

295.00-325.00

450.00-495.00
Leaded glass doors

350.00-395.00

275.00-295.00
Server

450.00-495.00

350.00-395.00

BUFFETS (sideboards)

The prices in this book represent the retail price range that a dealer might
ask for a fully restored and refinished piece of oak furniture.

650.00-900.00

500.00-600.00

4,000.00-6,000.00
Museum Quality

400.00-475.00

400.00-475.00

BUFFETS (sideboards)

The prices in this book represent the retail price range that a dealer might
ask for a fully restored and refinished piece of oak furniture.

550.00-650.00

500.00-600.00

550.00-650.00

400.00-450.00

450.00-750.00

BUFFETS (sideboards)

The prices in this book represent the retail price range that a dealer might
ask for a fully restored and refinished piece of oak furniture.

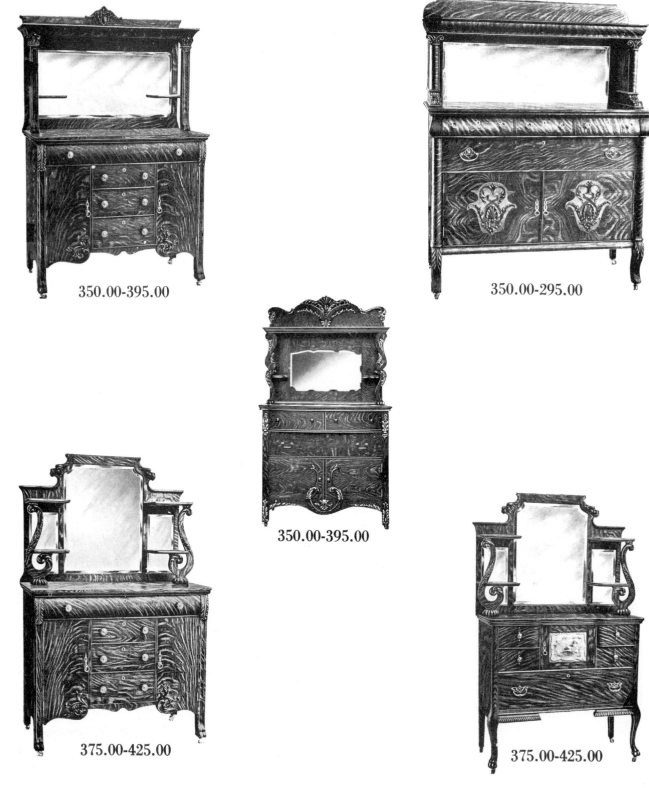

350.00-395.00

350.00-295.00

350.00-395.00

375.00-425.00

375.00-425.00

BUFFETS (sideboards)

The prices in this book represent the retail price range that a dealer might
ask for a fully restored and refinished piece of oak furniture.

325.00-375.00

325.00-375.00

375.00-475.00

350.00-450.00

225.00-275.00

350.00-400.00

300.00-350.00

BUFFETS (sideboards)

The prices in this book represent the retail price range that a dealer might
ask for a fully restored and refinished piece of oak furniture.

4,000-6,000
Museum Quality

BUFFETS (sideboards)

The prices in this book represent the retail price range that a dealer might
ask for a fully restored and refinished piece of oak furniture

450.00-650.00

325.00-425.00

350.00-450.00

450.00-600.00

700.00-1,000.00

BUFFETS (sideboards)

The prices in this book represent the retail price range that a dealer might
ask for a fully restored and refinished piece of oak furniture.

400.00-600.00

650.00-900.00

800.00-1,100.00

1,200.00-1,500.00

BUFFETS (sideboards)

The prices in this book represent the retail price range that a dealer might
ask for a fully restored and refinished piece of oak furniture.

650.00-800.00

500.00-700.00

800.00-1,100.00

400.00-600.00

CHINA BUFFETS

China Buffets are very rare. Their scarcity makes them popular items. They are excellent for displaying china and glassware.

500.00-550.00

500.00-550.00

1,000.00-1,250.00
Corner China
Buffet with leaded glass front
& beveled mirror in back.

500.00-600.00

475.00-550.00

600.00-700.00

600.00-700.00

CHAIRS
(Sets of Four)

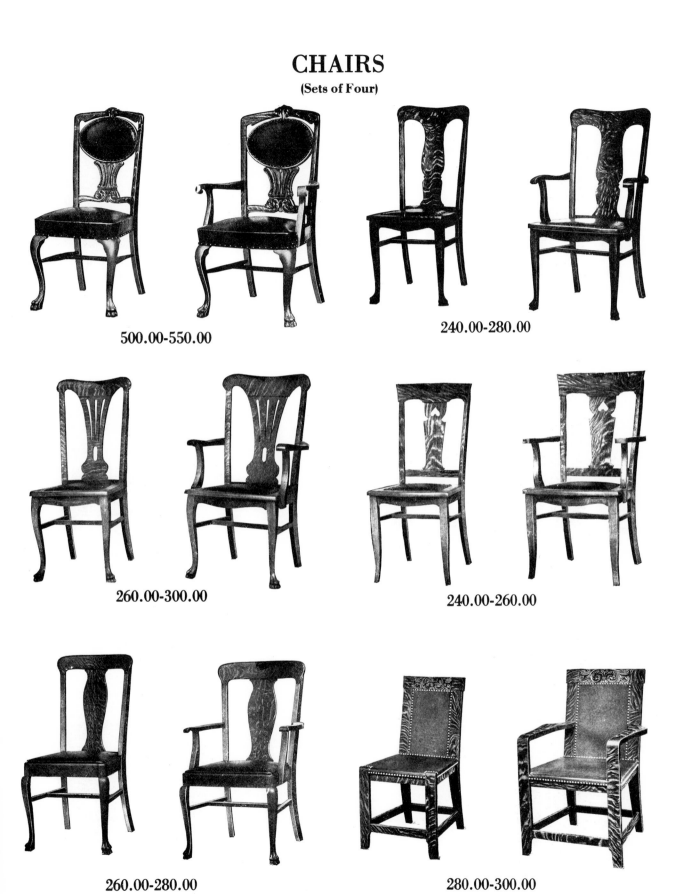

500.00-550.00

240.00-280.00

260.00-300.00

240.00-260.00

260.00-280.00

280.00-300.00

CHAIRS
(Sets of Four)

The prices in this book represent the retail price range that a dealer might ask for a fully restored and refinished piece of oak furniture.

500.00-525.00

420.00-460.00

375.00-425.00

240.00-260.00

280.00-320.00

300.00-320.00

200.00-250.00
Each
Office or Lounge
Chair

200.00-240.00

95.00-125.00 each.

CHAIRS

The prices in this book represent the retail price range that a dealer might
ask for a fully restored and refinished piece of oak furniture.

275.00-325.00

110.00-130.00

115.00-130.00

60.00

75.00

60.00

75.00

95.00-110.00

65.00-75.00

340.00-400.00
Sets of Four

CHAIRS

(Sets of four except when noted)
Chairs on this page
all have pressed cane bottoms.

280.00-320.00

90.00-110.00 each

75.00-95.00 each

280.00-320.00

260.00-280.00

350.00-400.00

320.00-340.00

220.00-240.00

300.00-320.00

350.00-400.00

350.00-400.00

350.00-400.00

360.00-410.00

CHAIRS
(Sets of Four)

300.00-350.00

300.00-350.00

220.00-260.00

320.00-380.00

CHAIRS

(Sets of Four)

260.00-280.00

210.00-240.00

300.00-350.00

200.00-225.00

200.00-225.00

220.00-250.00

CHAIRS
(Sets of Four except when noted)

250.00-300.00
Each

200.00-250.00
Each

225.00-275.00
Each

20.00-240.00

200.00-220.00

220.00-240.00

220.00-240.00

200.00-220.00

200.00-220.00

200.00-220.00

200.00-220.00

200.00-240.00

200.00-240.00

160.00-180.00

180.00-200.00

220.00-240.00

180.00-200.00

160.00-180.00

CHAIRS

(Sets of Four)

The prices in this book represent the retail price range that a dealer might
ask for a fully restored and refinished piece of oak furniture.

180.00-200.00

180.00-200.00

180.00-200.00

180.00-200.00

200.00-220.00

180.00-200.00

220.00-240.00
Shaker Style

240.00-280.00
Shaker Style

CHAIRS

(Sets of Four)

180.00-200.00

180.00-200.00

180.00-200.00

180.00-200.00

180.00-210.00

180.00-200.00

180.00-200.00

180.00-200.00

180.00-200.00

CHARS

The prices in this book represent the retail price range that a dealer might
ask for a fully restored and refinished piece of oak furniture.

900.00-1,200.00
3 Piece Set

100.00-125.00

75.00-85.00
Mission Style

100.00-125.00

175.00-200.00

CHAIRS
(Sets of Four)

250.00-300.00

275.00-300.00

275.00-300.00

210.00-230.00

220.00-240.00

220.00-240.00

CHAIRS

220.00-250.00

240.00-275.00

60.00-80.00

60.00-80.00

60.00-70.00

60.00-70.00

70.00-90.00

140.00-175.00

150.00-175.00

125.00-150.00

125.00-150.00

DESK CHAIRS

The prices in this book represent the retail price range that a dealer might
ask for a fully restored and refinished piece of oak furniture.

130.00-170.00

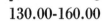

130.00-160.00

80.00-100.00

200.00-250.00

200.00-250.00

150.00-175.00

100.00-125.00

110.00-130.00

80.00-95.00

STOOLS

The prices in this book represent the retail price range that a dealer might
ask for a fully restored and refinished piece of oak furniture.

100.00-125.00

85.00-95.00

125.00-150.00

110.00-130.00

110.00-130.00

125.00-150.00

ROCKING CHAIRS

120.00-140.00

150.00-175.00

160.00-190.00

130.00-160.00

130.00-160.00

130.00-160.00

130.00-160.00

130.00-160.00

130.00-160.00

120.00-140.00

130.00-160.00

ROCKING CHAIRS

The prices in this book represent the retail price range that a dealer might
ask for a fully restored and refinished piece of oak furniture.

100.00-120.00

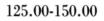

125.00-150.00

120.00-140.00

100.00-120.00

110.00-130.00

110.00-130.00

120.00-140.00

110.00-130.00

100.00-120.00

ROCKING CHAIRS

The prices in this book represent the retail price range that a dealer might
ask for a fully restored and refinished piece of oak furniture.

70.00-85.00

70.00-85.00

80.00-95.00

80.00-95.00

95.00-110.00

130.00-150.00

75.00-90.00

70.00-80.00

ROCKING CHAIRS

The prices in this book represent the retail price range that a dealer might
ask for a fully restored and refinished piece of oak furniture.

85.00-95.00

110.00-130.00
Sewing Rocker

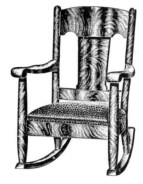

85.00-95.00

85.00-95.00

100.00-125.00

125.00-150.00

110.00-130.00

80.00-95.00

100.00-115.00

80.00-95.00

ROCKING CHAIRS

The prices in this book represent the retail price range that a dealer might
ask for a fully restored and refinished piece of oak furniture.

80.00-90.00

80.00-100.00

80.00-100.00

75.00-95.00

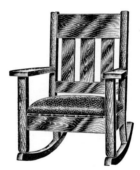

75.00-95.00

75.00-95.00

80.00-95.00

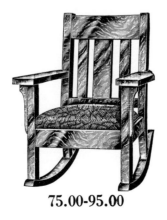

75.00-95.00

80.00-100.00

ROCKING CHAIRS

The prices in this book represent the retail price range that a dealer might
ask for a fully restored and refinished piece of oak furniture.

200.00-250.00   175.00-225.00   175.00-200.00

110.00-125.00   110.00-125.00

120.00-140.00   110.00-125.00   110.00-125.00

ROCKING CHAIRS

The prices in this book represent the retail price range that a dealer might
ask for a fully restored and refinished piece of oak furniture.

100.00-120.00

100.00-120.00

100.00-120.00

100.00-125.00

90.00-110.00

90.00-110.00

100.00-130.00

100.00-120.00

ROCKING CHAIRS

The prices in this book represent the retail price range that a dealer might
ask for a fully restored and refinished piece of oak furniture.

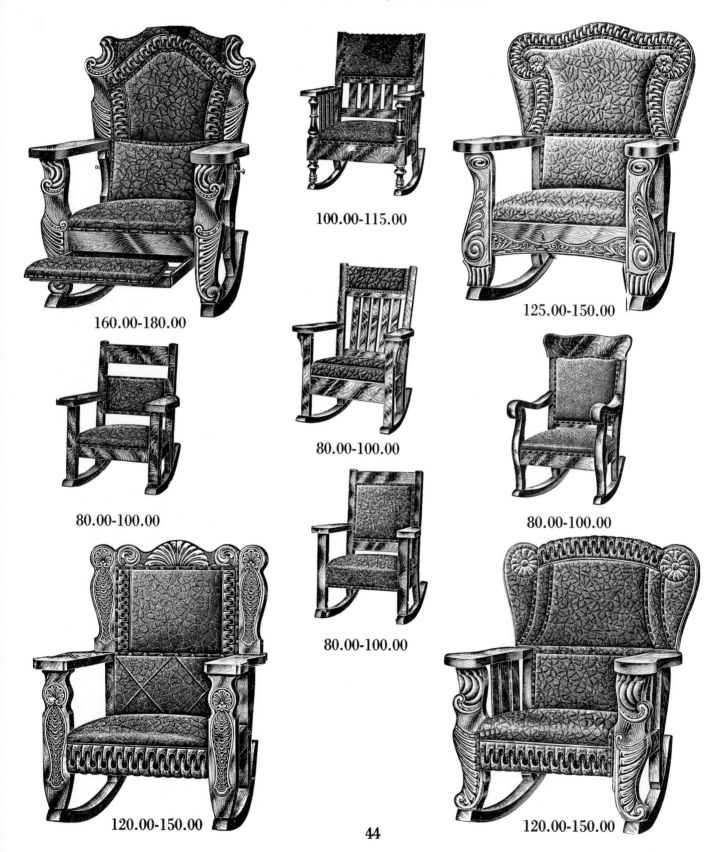

100.00-115.00

160.00-180.00

125.00-150.00

80.00-100.00

80.00-100.00

80.00-100.00

80.00-100.00

120.00-150.00

120.00-150.00

ROCKING CHAIRS

The prices in this book represent the retail price range that a dealer might
ask for a fully restored and refinished piece of oak furniture.

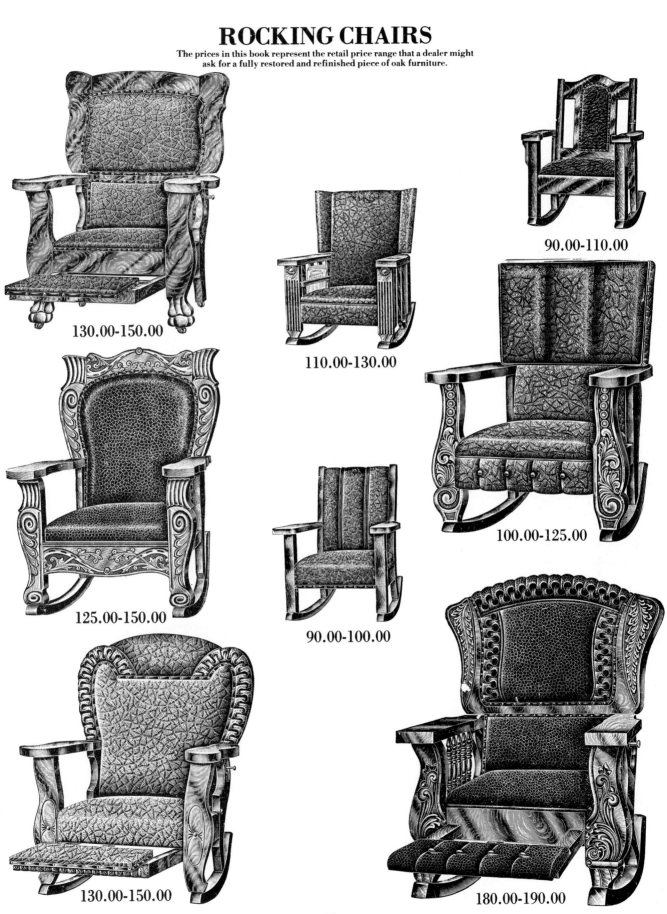

130.00-150.00

90.00-110.00

110.00-130.00

125.00-150.00

100.00-125.00

90.00-100.00

130.00-150.00

180.00-190.00

ROCKING CHAIRS

The prices in this book represent the retail price range that a dealer might
ask for a fully restored and refinished piece of oak furniture.

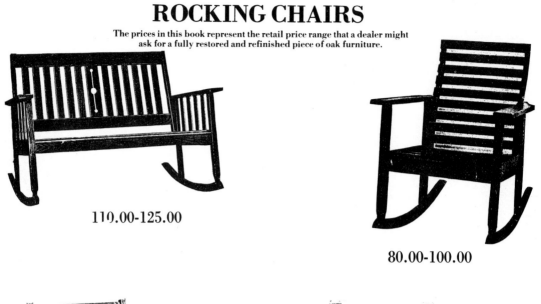

110.00-125.00

80.00-100.00

125.00-135.00

135.00-140.00

200.00-225.00

125.00-150.00

CHILDREN'S CHAIRS

The prices in this book represent the retail price range that a dealer might
ask for a fully restored and refinished piece of oak furniture.

125.00-150.00

120.00-140.00

120.00-140.00

120.00-140.00

115.00-130.00

125.00-150.00

225.00-250.00

130.00-160.00

85.00-105.00

75.00-85.00

85.00-95.00

120.00-140.00

CHILDREN'S CHAIRS

The prices in this book represent the retail price range that a dealer might
ask for a fully restored and refinished piece of oak furniture.

100.00-125.00   100.00-125.00   80.00-90.00

95.00-105.00

80.00-90.00

80.00-90.00

80.00-90.00

80.00-95.00   80.00-95.00   75.00-95.00

48

CHILDREN'S CHAIRS

The prices in this book represent the retail price range that a dealer might
ask for a fully restored and refinished piece of oak furniture.

90.00-110.00

70.00-80.00

90.00-110.00

70.00-80.00

125.00-150.00

125.00-150.00

65.00-75.00

70.00-85.00

CHIFFONIERS

The prices in this book represent the retail price range that a dealer might ask for a fully restored and refinished piece of oak furniture.

175.00-225.00

175.00-225.00

160.00-190.00

225.00-275.00

275.00-325.00

225.00-275.00

200.00-250.00

200.00-250.00

160.00-190.00

CHIFFONIERS

The prices in this book represent the retail price range that a dealer might
ask for a fully restored and refinished piece of oak furniture.

225.00-295.00

220.00-260.00

200.00-250.00

200.00-250.00

200.00-250.00

200.00-240.00

200.00-240.00

250.00-280.00

250.00-295.00

250.00-295.00

200.00-250.00

CHIFFOROBES

Chifforobes are generally poor sellers. They are rather plain pieces, poorly constructed with thin boards in drawers and end panels. The price for these has changed little in three years.

The prices in this book represent the retail price range that a dealer might ask for a fully restored and refinished piece of oak furniture.

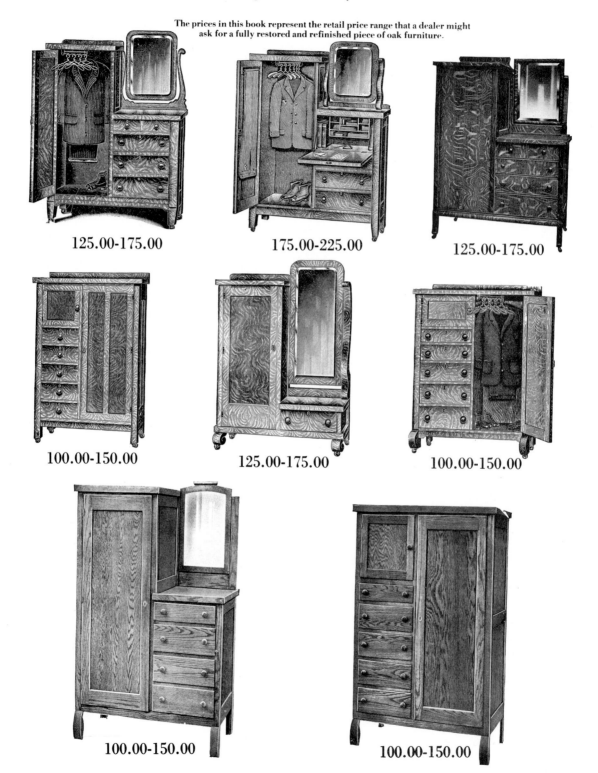

125.00-175.00

175.00-225.00

125.00-175.00

100.00-150.00

125.00-175.00

100.00-150.00

100.00-150.00

100.00-150.00

CHINA CABINETS

Oak china cabinets are the most sought-after items of the Golden Oak Period of furniture. They are being reproduced in great numbers due to the limited number of originals.

1,000.00-1,200.00

900.00-1,100.00

1,000.00-1,200.00

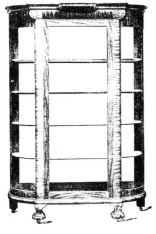

500.00-600.00

1,000-1,200.00

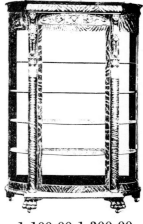

1,100.00-1,300.00

1,600.00-1,800.00

400.00-450.00

600.00-700.00

CHINA CABINETS

The prices in this book represent the retail price range that a dealer might
ask for a fully restored and refinished piece of oak furniture.

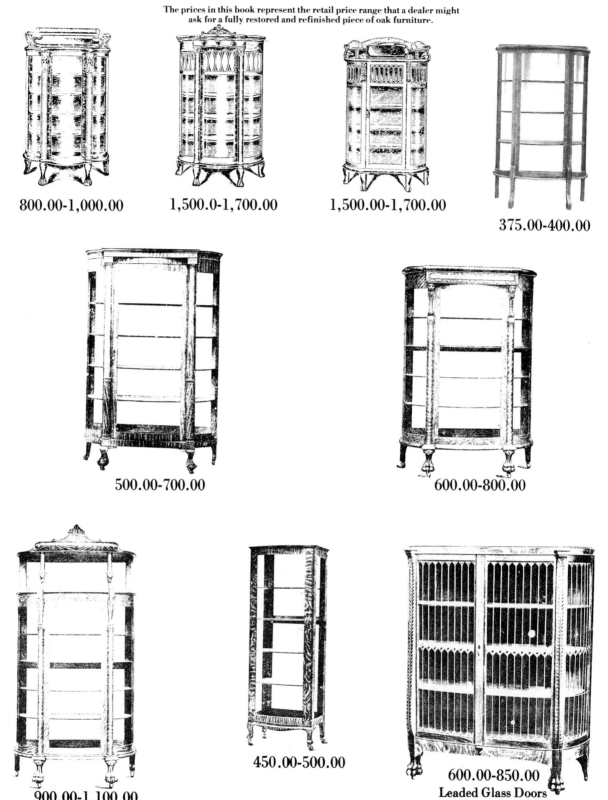

800.00-1,000.00

1,500.0-1,700.00

1,500.00-1,700.00

375.00-400.00

500.00-700.00

600.00-800.00

900.00-1,100.00

450.00-500.00

600.00-850.00
Leaded Glass Doors

CHINA CABINETS

The prices in this book represent the retail price range that a dealer might
ask for a fully restored and refinished piece of oak furniture.

750.00-850.00

600.00-700.00

600.00-700.00

600.00-800.00

400.00-600.00

500.00-600.00

500.00-600.00

CHINA CABINETS

The prices in this book represent the retail price range that a dealer might ask for a fully restored and refinished piece of oak furniture.

400.00-500.00

400.00-500.00

400.00-500.00

400.00-500.00

500.00-600.00

300.00-400.00

56

CHINA CABINETS

The prices in this book represent the retail price range that a dealer might
ask for a fully restored and refinished piece of oak furniture.

600.00-750.00

600.00-700.00
leaded glass

1,100.00-1,300.00
Corner Cabinet
(Very Rare)

700.00-800.00
Corner Cabinet
(Very Rare)

CHINA CABINETS

The prices in this book represent the retail price range that a dealer might
ask for a fully restored and refinished piece of oak furniture.

300.00-350.00

300.00-350.00

350.00-400.00

250.00-275.00

300.00-350.00

CLOCKS, KITCHEN

The prices in this book represent the retail price range that a dealer might
ask for a fully restored and refinished piece of oak furniture.

150.00-175.00

125.00-150.00

125.00-150.00

125.00-150.00

150.00-175.00

125.00-150.00

125.00-150.00

125.00-150.00

175.00-195.00

125.00-150.00

200.00-225.00

59

CLOCKS, KITCHEN

The prices in this book represent the retail price range that a dealer might
ask for a fully restored and refinished piece of oak furniture.

150.00-175.00

275.00-325.00

130.00-160.00

125.00-150.00

175.00-200.00

175.00-200.00

175.00-200.00

160.00-180.00

125.00-150.00

CLOCKS, WALL

The prices in this book represent the retail price range that a dealer might
ask for a fully restored and refinished piece of oak furniture.

300.00-350.00

250.00-300.00

200.00-250.00

350.00-400.00

350.00-400.00

350.00-400.00

CLOCKS, WALL

The prices in this book represent the retail price range that a dealer might
ask for a fully restored and refinished piece of oak furniture.

250.00-300.00

250.00-300.00

225.00-275.00

225.00-275.00

225.00-275.00

225.00-275.00

CLOCKS

The prices in this book represent the retail price range that a dealer might
ask for a fully restored and refinished piece of oak furniture.

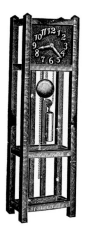

450.00-500.00
Mission
Grandfather Clock

125.00-150.00

125.00-150.00

125.00-150.00

150.00-175.00

125.00-150.00

450.00-500.00
Mission
Grandfather Clock

COUCHES

The prices in this book represent the retail price range that a dealer might
ask for a fully restored and refinished piece of oak furniture.

450.00-500.00

475.00-525.00

450.00-500.00

425.00-450.00

450.00-500.00

425.00-450.00

425.00-450.00

COUCHES

The prices in this book represent the retail price range that a dealer might
ask for a fully restored and refinished piece of oak furniture.

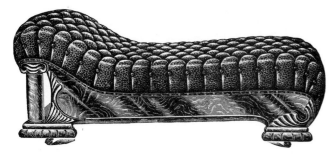

425.00-475.00

400.00-425.00

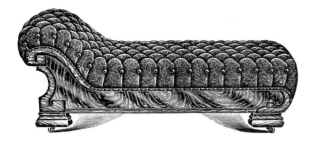

400.00-425.00

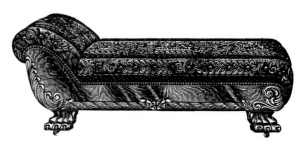

450.00-475.00

475.00-500.00

525.00-575.00

450.00-495.00

450.00-495.00

COUCHES

450.00-475.00

325.00-350.00

400.00-450.00

325.00-350.00

325.00-350.00

250.00-300.00

DAVENPORTS

The prices in this book represent the retail price range that a dealer might
ask for a fully restored and refinished piece of oak furniture.

250.00-280.00

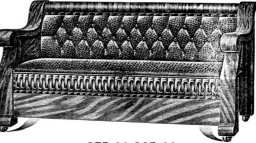

275.00-325.00

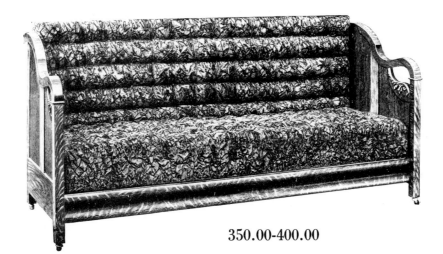

350.00-400.00

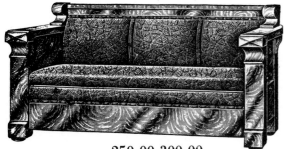

250.00-300.00

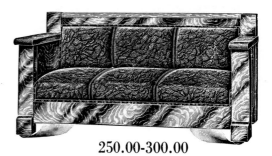

250.00-300.00

DAVENPORTS

The prices in this book represent the retail price range that a dealer might
ask for a fully restored and refinished piece of oak furniture.

275.00-325.00

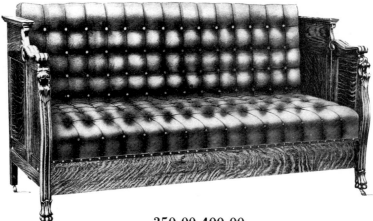

350.00-400.00

275.00-325.00

325.00-375.00

DESKS

The prices in this book represent the retail price range that a dealer might
ask for a fully restored and refinished piece of oak furniture.

400.00-450.00

200.00-250.00

250.00-275.00

275.00-325.00

200.00-250.00

240.00-275.00

220.00-240.00

250.00-275.00

DESKS

300.00-350.00

400.00-450.00

3,500.00-4,500.00
Museum Quality

300.00-325.00

325.00-350.00

325.00-375.00

275.00-300.00

275.00-300.00

275.00-300.00

DESKS

The prices in this book represent the retail price range that a dealer might ask for a fully restored and refinished piece of oak furniture.

1,500.00-1,800.00
"Waterfall"
or "S" Roll Top

1,200.00-1,500.00
Secretary Desk

550.00-650.00

800.00-900.00

1,200.00-1,500.00
Waterfall Roll Top

71

1,700.00-2,000.00
Waterfall Roll Top

DESKS

1,200.00-1,500.00
Waterfall Roll Top

350.00-400.00

900.00-1,100.00
Waterfall Roll Top

500.00-600.00

1,200.00-1,500.00

550.00-650.00

DESKS

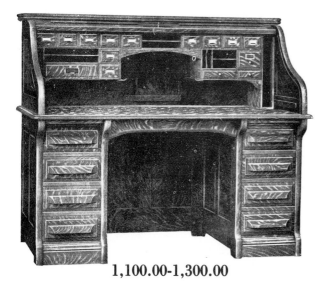

1,100.00-1,300.00

350.00-400.00

900.00-1,100.00
Waterfall Roll Top

350.00-400.00

500.00-550.00

300.00-350.00

DESKS

225.00-275.00

225.00-250.00

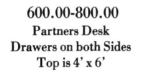

600.00-800.00
Partners Desk
Drawers on both Sides
Top is 4' x 6'

125.00-150.00

225.00-275.00

DESKS

500.00-600.00

225.00-250.00
Mission

225.00-250.00
Mission

140.00-160.00
Mission

200.00-250.00
Mission

140.00-160.00
Mission

175.00-225.00

275.00-300.00

DESKS

350.00-400.00
Stand Up Desk

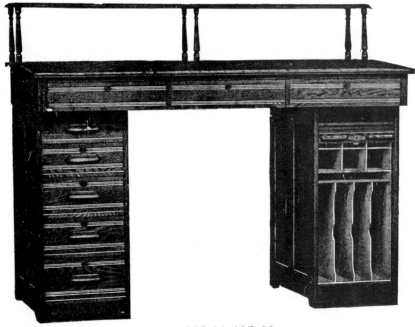

375.00-425.00
Stand Up Desk

BOOKCASE DESKS

The prices in this book represent the retail price range that a dealer might
ask for a fully restored and refinished piece of oak furniture.

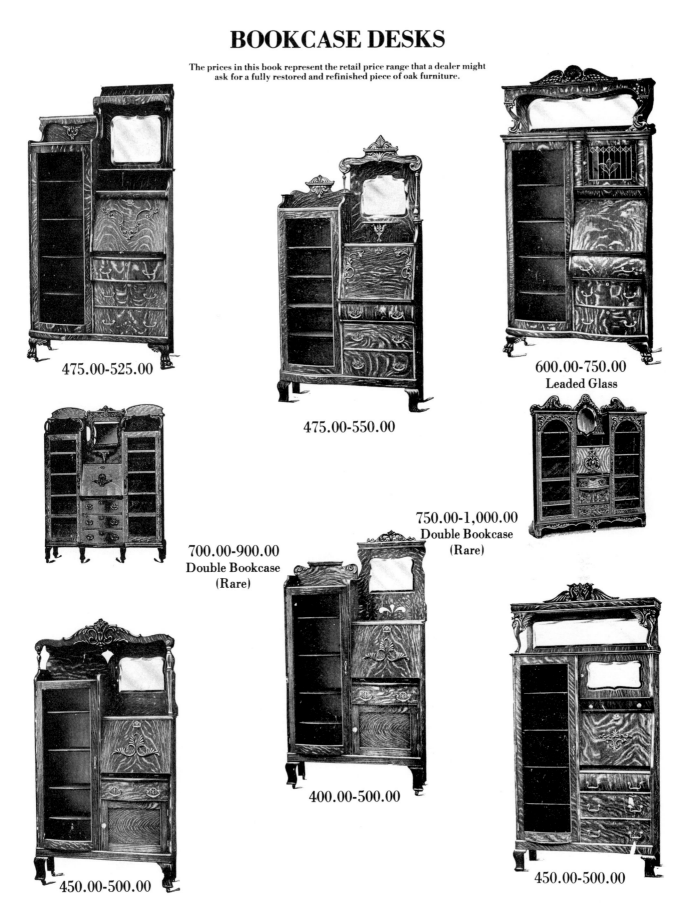

475.00-525.00

475.00-550.00

600.00-750.00
Leaded Glass

750.00-1,000.00
Double Bookcase
(Rare)

700.00-900.00
Double Bookcase
(Rare)

400.00-500.00

450.00-500.00

450.00-500.00

BOOKCASE DESKS

The prices in this book represent the retail price range that a dealer might ask for a fully restored and refinished piece of oak furniture.

325.00-375.00

300.00-350.00

350.00-400.00

375.00-450.00

375.00-450.00

350.00-395.00

350.00-395.00

450.00-550.00

375.00-450.00

DRESSERS

The prices in this book represent the retail price range that a dealer might
ask for a fully restored and refinished piece of oak furniture.

225.00-250.00

150.00-175.00

250.00-275.00

150.00-170.00

125.00-150.00

125.00-150.00

150.00-175.00

DRESSERS

The prices in this book represent the retail price range that a dealer might ask for a fully restored and refinished piece of oak furniture.

225.00-250.00

150.00-175.00

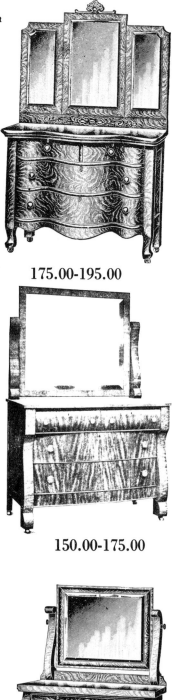

175.00-195.00

225.00-250.00

175.00-195.00

150.00-175.00

125.00-150.00

175.00-195.00

150.00-175.00

DRESSERS

The prices in this book represent the retail price range that a dealer might
ask for a fully restored and refinished piece of oak furniture.

200.00-225.00

150.00-175.00

150.00-175.00

150.00-175.00

150.00-175.00

175.00-200.00

160.00-185.00

150.00-175.00

175.00-200.00

200.00-225.00

200.00-225.00

200.00-225.00

DRESSERS

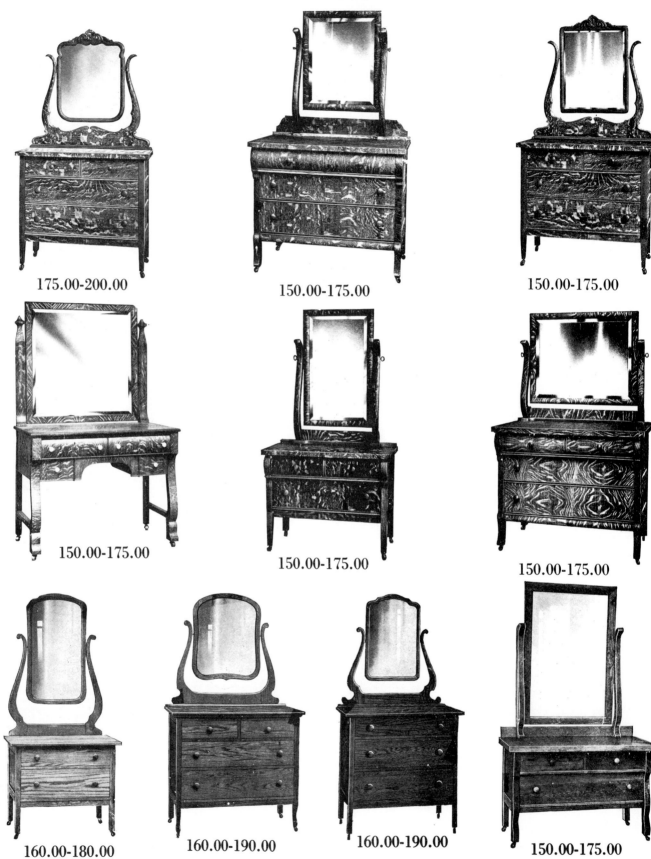

175.00-200.00

150.00-175.00

150.00-175.00

150.00-175.00

150.00-175.00

150.00-175.00

160.00-180.00

160.00-190.00

160.00-190.00

150.00-175.00

DRESSERS

The prices in this book represent the retail price range that a dealer might
ask for a fully restored and refinished piece of oak furniture.

225.00-250.00

180.00-200.00

160.00-180.00

180.00-200.00

150.00-170.00

200.00-225.00

140.00-160.00

160.00-180.00

HALL RACKS & HALL TREES

The prices in this book represent the retail price range that a dealer might
ask for a fully restored and refinished piece of oak furniture.

80.00-95.00

550.00-650.00

500.00-600.00

450.00-550.00

600.00-800.00

HALL RACKS & HALL TREES

The prices in this book represent the retail price range that a dealer might
ask for a fully restored and refinished piece of oak furniture.

500.00-600.00

.00-<

475.00-525.00

400.00-450.00

600.00-750.00

HALL RACKS & HALL TREES

The prices in this book represent the retail price range that a dealer might ask for a fully restored and refinished piece of oak furniture.

350.00-400.00

300.00-350.00

375.00-425.00

325.00-375.00

325.00-375.00

350.00-400.00

425.00-325.00

HALL RACKS & HALL TREES

The prices in this book represent the retail price range that a dealer might
ask for a fully restored and refinished piece of oak furniture.

525.00-625.00

350.00-400.00

325.00-350.00

300.00-350.00

300.00-325.00

275.00-295.00

300.00-325.00

450.00-550.00

500.00-600.00

450.00-550.00

ICE BOXES

The prices in this book represent the retail price range that a dealer might
ask for a fully restored and refinished piece of oak furniture.

Ice boxes for home use came in
four basic sizes: 25 lb., 50 lb., 75
lb., and 100 lb. Ice box prices on
the West Coast are much higher
than the rest of the U.S.

250.00-325.00

250.00-325.00

250.00-325.00

⌄25.00
250.00-325.00

250.00-325.00

400:00-500.00

ICE BOXES

The prices in this book represent the retail price range that a dealer might
ask for a fully restored and refinished piece of oak furniture.

200.00-225.00

250.00-325.00

200.00-225.00

250.00-325.00

250.00-325.00

KITCHEN CABINETS

The prices in this book represent the retail price range that a dealer might
ask for a fully restored and refinished piece of oak furniture.

350.00-395.00

375.00-425.00

350.00-395.00

350.00-395.00

375.00-425.00

350.00-395.00

350.00-395.00

350.00-395.00

450.00-500.00

CUPBOARDS

275.00-325.00

350.00-395.00

300.00-350.00

300.00-350.00

300.00-350.00

WARDROBES

The prices in this book represent the retail price range that a dealer might
ask for a fully restored and refinished piece of oak furniture.

125.00-175.00

175.00-225.00

225.00-275.00

300.00-375.00

MIRRORS

The prices in this book represent the retail price range that a dealer might
ask for a fully restored and refinished piece of oak furniture.

200.00-250.00

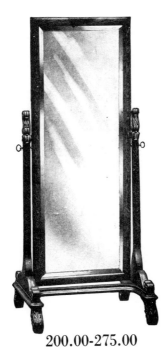

200.00-275.00

180.00-210.00

200.00-250.00

300.00-350.00

425.00-500.00

TABLES, ROUND

The prices in this book represent the retail price range that a dealer might
ask for a fully restored and refinished piece of oak furniture.

550.00-650.00

600.00-700.00

450.00-550.00

400.00-475.00

450.00-550.00

350.00-400.00

TABLES, ROUND

The prices in this book represent the retail price range that a dealer might
ask for a fully restored and refinished piece of oak furniture.

500.00-600.00

500.00-600.00

450.00-550.00

650.00-850.00

500.00-600.00

500.00-600.00

TABLES, ROUND

The prices in this book represent the retail price range that a dealer might
ask for a fully restored and refinished piece of oak furniture.

325.00-400.00

250.00-300.00

450.00-475.00

400.00-450.00

400.00-450.00

500.00-600.00

TABLES, ROUND

The prices in this book represent the retail price range that a dealer might
ask for a fully restored and refinished piece of oak furniture.

400.00-500.00

400.00-475.00

450.00-550.00

300.00-350.00

325.00-375.00

250.00-300.00

325.00-400.00

1,000.00-1,200.00
(Museum Quality)

TABLES, ROUND

The prices in this book represent the retail price range that a dealer might
ask for a fully restored and refinished piece of oak furniture.

250.00-300.00

250.00-300.00

250.00-300.00

250.00-300.00

TABLES, ROUND

The prices in this book represent the retail price range that a dealer might
ask for a fully restored and refinished piece of oak furniture.

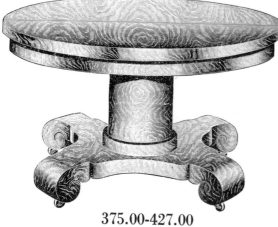

375.00-427.00

300.00-350.00

250.00-295.00

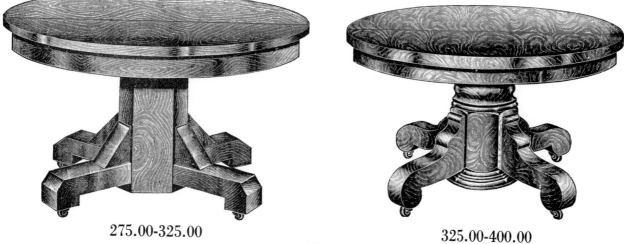

275.00-325.00

325.00-400.00

TABLES, ROUND

The prices in this book represent the retail price range that a dealer might
ask for a fully restored and refinished piece of oak furniture.

350.00-425.00

400.00-450.00

350.00-425.00

375.00-450.00

TABLES, ROUND

The prices in this book represent the retail price range that a dealer might
ask for a fully restored and refinished piece of oak furniture.

300.00-350.00

275.00-325.00

300.00-350.00

350.00-425.00

275.00-325.00

250.00-295.00

225.00-275.00

225.00-250.00

250.00-295.00

TABLES, SQUARE

275.00-325.00

275.00-325.00

275.00-325.00

425.00-475.00

225.00-275.00

TABLES, SQUARE

150.00-190.00

150.00-190.00

200.00-250.00

250.00-300.00

150.00-190.00

225.00-275.00

175.00-225.00

175.00-225.00

TABLES, SQUARE

The prices in this book represent the retail price range that a dealer might
ask for a fully restored and refinished piece of oak furniture.

150.00-175.00

400.00-450.00

150.00-175.00

175.00-200.00

250.00-295.00

TABLES, SQUARE

The prices in this book represent the retail price range that a dealer might
ask for a fully restored and refinished piece of oak furniture.

100.00-125.00

100.00-125.00

100.00-125.00

85.00-110.00

90.00-110.00

70.00-100.00

125.00-150.00

130.00-150.00

TABLES, LIBRARY

The prices in this book represent the retail price range that a dealer might
ask for a fully restored and refinished piece of oak furniture.

150.00-175.00

175.00-200.00

125.00-150.00

150.00-175.00

100.00-150.00

115.00-140.00

TABLES, LIBRARY

The prices in this book represent the retail price range that a dealer might
ask for a fully restored and refinished piece of oak furniture.

3,000.00-4,000.00
(Museum Quality)

350.00-450.00

175.00-200.00

200.00-250.00

200.00-250.00

TABLES, LIBRARY

The prices in this book represent the retail price range that a dealer might
ask for a fully restored and refinished piece of oak furniture.

200.00-250.00

175.00-225.00

200.00-250.00

200.00-250.00

250.00-300.00

175.00-195.00

200.00-225.00

TABLES, LIBRARY

The prices in this book represent the retail price range that a dealer might ask for a fully restored and refinished piece of oak furniture.

150.00-175.00

125.00-150.00

125.00-150.00

200.00-250.00

TABLES, LIBRARY

The prices in this book represent the retail price range that a dealer might
ask for a fully restored and refinished piece of oak furniture.

350.00-400.00

200.00-225.00

TABLES, LIBRARY

The prices in this book represent the retail price range that a dealer might
ask for a fully restored and refinished piece of oak furniture.

175.00-200.00

200.00-225.00

150.00-175.00

125.00-150.00

125.00-150.00

100.00-125.00

125.00-150.00

200.00-250.00

TABLES, STAND

The prices in this book represent the retail price range that a dealer might ask for a fully restored and refinished piece of oak furniture.

150.00-175.00
Checkerboard
Inlay

100.00-125.00

100.00-125.00

75.00-100.00

75.00-95.00

70.00-90.00

85.00-110.00

70.00-85.00

90.00-110.00

100.00-125.00
Inlaid Top

80.00-100.00

70.00-90.00

65.00-80.00

85.00-100.00

75.00-85.00

TABLES, END

The prices in this book represent the retail price range that a dealer might ask for a fully restored and refinished piece of oak furniture.

125.00-150.00

80.00-100.00

70.00-80.00

50.00-60.00

75.00-85.00

75.00-85.00

90.00-110.00

45.00-55.00

70.00-80.00

60.00-70.00

TABLES, END

The prices in this book represent the retail price range that a dealer might
ask for a fully restored and refinished piece of oak furniture.

90.00-110.00

70.00-80.00

70.00-90.00

70.00-90.00

60.00-70.00

50.00-60.00

60.00-70.00

50.00-60.00

175.00-200.00

50.00-60.00

70.00-80.00

75.00-95.00

100.00-120.00

WASHSTANDS

The prices in this book represent the retail price range that a dealer might ask for a fully restored and refinished piece of oak furniture.

175.00-195.00

160.00-180.00

175.00-195.00

120.00-140.00

140.00-170.00

120.00-150.00

160.00-185.00

175.00-195.00

150.00-175.00

200.00-235.00

200.00-235.00

WASHSTANDS

The prices in this book represent the retail price range that a dealer might
ask for a fully restored and refinished piece of oak furniture.

150.00-175.00   150.00-175.00   150.00-175.00   175.00-195.00

150.00-175.00   200.00-235.00   200.00-235.00   175.00-200.00

175.00-200.00   175.00-200.00

BARBER SHOP FIXTURES

The prices in this book represent the retail price range that a dealer might
ask for a fully restored and refinished piece of oak furniture.

250.00-300.00

250.00-300.00

300.00-350.00

2,000-3,000.00

250.00-295.00

125.00-150.00

MEDICINE CABINETS

75.00-95.00

75.00-95.00

60.00-80.00

160.00-190.00

MIRRORS, HANGING

The prices in this book represent the retail price range that a dealer might ask for a fully restored and refinished piece of oak furniture.

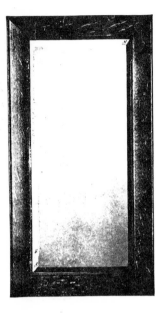

125.00-150.00

30.00-45.00

75.00-95.00

60.00-80.00

80.00-100.00

85.00-100.00

85.00-100.00

FILE BOXES

225.00-275.00

300.00-400.00

450.00-550.00

MUSIC CABINETS

The prices in this book represent the retail price range that a dealer might ask for a fully restored and refinished piece of oak furniture.

125.00-150.00

100.00-125.00

125.00-150.00

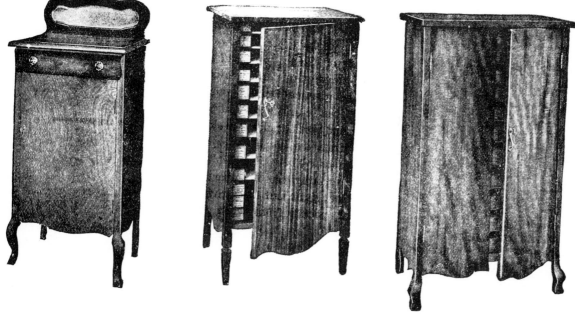

125.00-150.00

100.00-125.00

125.00-150.00

PEDESTALS

The prices in this book represent the retail price range that a dealer might ask for a fully restored and refinished piece of oak furniture.

60.00-70.00

90.00-110.00

70.00-90.00

50.00-60.00

30.00-40.00

50.00-75.00

40.00-50.00

35.00-45.00

35.00-50.00

125.00-150.00

100.00-125.00

300.00-350.00
(Pedestal Bar)

WASHING MACHINES

The prices in this book represent the retail price range that a dealer might
ask for a fully restored and refinished piece of oak furniture.

250.00-300.00

300.00-350.00

250.00-300.00

300.00-350.00

ODDS & ENDS

The prices in this book represent the retail price range that a dealer might
ask for a fully restored and refinished piece of oak furniture.

80.00-95.00

90.00-110.00

150.00-195.00

125.00-150.00

125.00-150.00

75.00-95.00

75.00-95.00

95.00-125.00

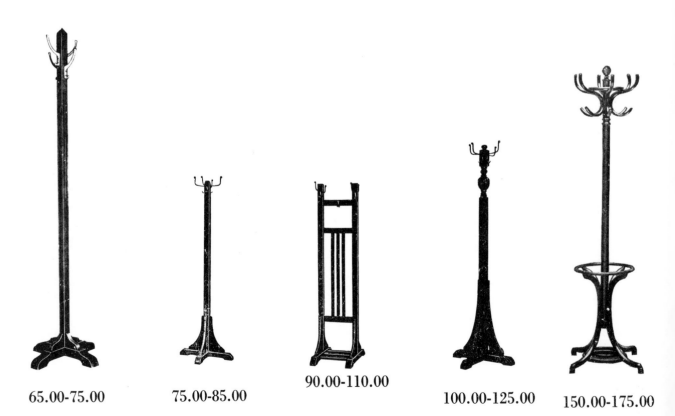

65.00-75.00

75.00-85.00

90.00-110.00

100.00-125.00

150.00-175.00

INDEX

OTHER BOOKS FOR COLLECTORS

All Priced and Illustrated

Standard Antique Clock Value Guide $11.95

Antique Wicker Furniture — Conover Hill 6.95

Encyclopedia of Akro Agate Glass — Florence 8.95

Millersburg Carnival Glass — Edwards 8.95

The Standard Cut Glass Value Guide — Evers 8.95

Glass Candlesticks — Archer 7.95

Modern Collector's Dolls I — Smith — Hardbound 17.95

Modern Collector's Dolls II — Smith — Hardbound 17.95

Modern Collector's Dolls III — Smith — Hardbound 17.95

Antique Collector's Dolls — Smith — Hardbound 17.95

Antique Collector's Dolls II — Smith — Hardbound 17.95

Armand Marseille Dolls — Smith 7.95

1,000 Fruit Jars III — Schroeder 4.95

Antique Tools — Hill 6.95

Early American Primitives — Hill 6.95

Flea Market Trader 5.95

Standard Antique Dolls 7.95

Standard Modern Dolls 7.95

Roseville Pottery — Huxford — Hardbound 17.95

Encyclopedia of Fiesta — Huxford 7.95

Collector's Encyclopedia of Depression Glass 14.95

ORDER FROM YOUR FAVORITE DEALER
OR
COLLECTOR BOOKS
Box 3009
Paducah, Kentucky 42001